THE REBIRTH OF A PHOENIX

THE REBIRTH OF A PHOENIX

A Poetry Collection

DESTINEE SHIPLEY

Ariel Chapman

Firebird Spark, LLC

Published by Firebird Spark, LLC

First Printing, 2022

Cover art by Ariel Chapman

For everyone on the journey of self-discovery

Contents

3
RISING

Preface

I wrote these poems
These stories
Streams of Consciousness
Because my brain needed an outlet
And simply talking wasn't going to cut it
My journals were all filling up with my thoughts
And I knew that
There were more people in the world
Besides just me
Who can relate to what I'm saying here
This is a coming-of-age story
This is the story of a phoenix
Born
Fallen
And rising again

I

Beginnings

Little Flames

I had to begin somewhere
For there is nowhere I can go but forward
After that

This is the glimpse into the mind
Of a baby bird
Just finding its wings

Misconceptions

I am not all that I seem
There's more to me that meets the eye
Do not misunderstand the vibes you might be getting
I'm not just a highly intelligent beautiful Black face
I'm not only a purple loving saxophone playing swimmer
I'm beyond a Rubik's cube solving chess playing goody goody
Just because I cry for things doesn't mean I'm weak
Just because I hold my tongue doesn't make me afraid
Just because I'm out of the circle doesn't confirm I'm not listening
I am blessed and highly favored, for I am a child of God
I am strong and I am powerful,
And I am not one to be reckoned with
Don't expect me to fall neatly into social "norms"
I will not suppress my individuality and uniqueness
To cower away from everyone else
I no longer care that I am different
I no longer care that you have misconceptions
I no longer care what you say about me
You should get to know me,
For I am not all that I seem

I. AM. UNSTOPPABLE.

Unstoppable

Never take your eyes off your target
Or you'll lose it
Keep pushing to the end
Go above and beyond
No matter what is said
About you
And no matter who says it
Forget them
You've got places to go
You've got things to do
You've got people to meet
You've got games to win
When you realize who you are
For yourself
You will be unstoppable
That's what I heard
Repeating
And repeating again
In my head
And I thought
What is unstoppable?
Unstoppable is fighting the good fight
Win or lose
You die trying

Hesitation does not exist
Because there is no need
To hold back
I have what it takes
Knocked down by waves of can'ts
Kept down by won'ts
Just getting back up
Over
And over
Is defiance
Is showing the world that I
Can do anything
I have confidence in myself
And my own abilities
Almost makes me a little bit
Stubborn
Knowing that I can
That I should
That I will
Win
You think you've finished me
Convinced yourself that I
Can no longer move forward
But
You fail to realize
That the only way
ONLY WAY to stop me
Is to ensure that I am brain dead
So I can no longer think
No longer motivate myself
But nevertheless
It's not about proving myself
To you
I prove to me

Everyday, in everything
And everywhere I go
I am
UNSTOPPABLE

Personality

In terms of morals, I have several, but for every one of them, I stick to them and I stick to them strongly. I always try to stay firmly rooted in my beliefs and values—I guess that makes me a little stubborn. I am, however, able to see multiple perspectives of an argument. I'm proud, yet always try to be humble.

I always think things through, but many of my initial assumptions/reactions are based on emotion. I'm a very emotional person: I sympathize/empathize easily, sometimes I wear my heart on my sleeve, and I cry (not "easily", but I do cry). I am an optimist and always try to see the best in people and situations, but I'm not naive to negativity. I can become jealous of others, and I'm not a fan of things not going my way. I'm confident in many things, but not all. I tend to want affirmation from others about what I already know, but I'm gradually getting away from that.

Overall, I'm the caring, helpful type, the good listener, insightful, intelligent.

Survival

Survival:

Like swimming in dangerous waters or something

You're a swimmer. Survive

Survival can either mean going back to the shallow end, or learning to adapt to the dangerous waters so they are not as dangerous....

Exactly

How are u as a survivor

Well—aware of danger, but always able to adapt. I have to be, cuz it's survival of the fittest

I can't only limit myself to what is comfortable if I ever expect to grow

Hahahahaha

Lol what? You like my stream of consciousness?

Yea. Plz continue

Ok..hmm. Learning to survive can only be done through surviving itself. You can only learn to swim by swimming. There are no shortcuts. The shallow end is where you start, but you never want to end up there. It's a sign of stunted growth.

Ok

Even if it's the easiest way, it's still limiting myself. As I said, I am unstoppable. That means I cannot let fear of danger stop me from facing it. Taking risks is just a part of life. Ok now I'm done.

You have to risk big to gain the biggest rewards

Exactly

So you're a gambler?

I'm more of a gambler now than I was.

Is that good?

Yes, because I'm less afraid of what life throws at me. Instead of sitting idly by, I'm doing something with my life. Besides: My deepest fear is not that I am inadequate. My deepest fear is that I am powerful beyond measure. I let fear of the unknown stop me.

That's not to say I'm no longer cautious, but I am less likely to talk myself out of whatever I set in my mind to do if the benefit outweighs the cost

Not Knowing

It's getting down to the wire
It's almost that time
To step up
And step out
To be that exception
To the rule

But I'm scared
(Yeah, I'll admit it)
Scared I won't have what it takes
Scared of what is to be
Because I cannot see
The things that lie in store
Waiting for me

The world is full of challenges
And trials and tribulations
I know that through Him I can do all things
But I let the fear of the unknown
Take over the control of me

In the back of my mind
A voice keeps nagging
Telling me

That the worst part of a process
Is in the fear of not knowing

But in reality
If I'm too scared
To journey into the unknown
To do what I was *destined* to do
Then I've essentially failed myself

My goal is to keep on striving
And keep struggling
To live up to my full potential
Because there is a long road ahead

I do not yet know
What that road holds
But I can't let that stop me now
I've already begun

Stars

Stargazing
Looking up in the vast sky
And being able to say
Those are your stars
You know them all

The ones closest to you
Are the brightest
And the prettiest to look at
And the ones further away
Still have a beauty of their own
Both are there
And give depth and beauty
To the sky

When you leave that place
Where you always went stargazing
You know
That you will still see
All of your stars
In the new place you end up
Well
You hope
That you will see

All your stars

In reality
Some of the distant stars
Start to fade away
In the city lights
And the brighter ones
Start to lose some of their luster
And you see less and less stars
Until you can only see
The ones formerly the brightest
Now just dim pinpoints of light
Far far away

And suddenly new stars show up
Against the city lights
Shining bright
Right there
With you
Behind those stars
Your dull pinpoints
Are much harder to see
You love looking at the new stars
And the new constellations
But what about the others?
You knew
Well you thought you knew
You would always see them

But you don't have to always see
Your other stars
And the dimness
Is only a trick of the light
When you return to your place

For stargazing
You discover that your stars
Are just as bright as before
They are still there
Your stars will always be there
Even if you cannot see them
Whether through clouds
Or by the city lights
They are always there

Two EE's

As a child I've never had trouble spelling my own name
D-E-S-T-I-N-E-E ...Destinee
Eight letters
My teachers always had trouble though
They'd misread my name and make up their own:
"Desiree?.....Desiree Shipley?"
"Oh...that's me...it's Destinee"
I never understood that
I've been called Desiree on so many occasions
I *actually* answer to it when it's called
People misspell my name too
There are two EEs at the end of it
Not the generic Y that presses everyone into the same mold
And gives others pseudo-intuition
To who I am and what I stand for
People give me names that are not my own
And give me characteristics that are not my own
A backstory that is not mine
My name is my brand
My name is unique
I am unique
See I'm what you call a hidden gem
Not many people see me for the beautiful wonder
That lies within

They see Desiree at first glance
A girl that is not so uncommon, a generic girl
A girl who has nothing to offer but an "interesting name"
They hear Destiny with a Y
A pretty name, but a spelling so commonplace
That it has lost some of its luster
People assume that they know me
Because they *think* they know my name
But they are sadly mistaken
There is no R in Destinee
(so where they get Desiree, I don't know)
But there IS a T
A T that stands tall and proud
With arms outstretched like the cross on which my savior died
The savior who has carried me through the tough times
Like the God who made me who I am
Who gave me my talents
Who made me SPECIAL
The two EEs bring the letters in my name to an even 8
And the sight of them elongate my name
And allow it to roll off the tongue
Like water that rolls off a swimmer's back
Or the sweet melodies that spill forth from a saxophone: Destinee

If they had unearthed me
And explored the recesses of my personality
They would have seen the beautiful young woman I've become
They would have seen the talents
And the dedication and the drive
My passion for the things and the people I love
They would have seen the quirkiness
The silliness
The seriousness
They would have unearthed a gem

One that was formed in secret
That was made whole by time and pressure
Not a perfect gem, not by a long shot
But one that needs no alteration
That doesn't need to fit a particular mold
That can stand on its own and not crumble

Destinee
It means fate
It means I can choose who I want to be

2

Ashes

Dark Places

Spiraling out of control
Drowning in self doubt
And self-destruction
Buried here is my darkness

Trigger warning: this next section of writings contains themes and depictions of mental illness, suicidality, and abuse

Cold Night

I'm really cold. It must be fifty or sixty degrees...meaning its cold. Swinging back and forth in the crisp night air doesn't help me get any warmer. The frigidity pierces my thin jacket, right to tips of my fingers and the ends of my toes. It's silent save some frogs and bugs and the groups of nocturnal students milling around. My swing respects the silence and doesn't creak or moan. On my way over here I was thinking about stuff, life, love. Before I started walking I was on another swing doing the same. But here I don't really think. I just am. I look up and see the stars, just like the ones in my poem. Everything is dark but there are lights in the dorms and the stars light the sky and the moon casts a silvery glow—along with the lamps that line the walkways. Everyone is with someone tonight. But I felt I needed to come be by myself and reflect...I like it.

After the Love is Gone

Our world has lost its mind
(No really, we've lost it)
We've lost all humanity
We've lost all trust
We've lost all faith
And most of us have lost all hope
We are killing ourselves

Why is it that every time I turn on the news
There has been *another* bombing in Pakistan
Another bombing in Israel
Why
A deadly outbreak in Africa
That nobody but a handful of Americans received treatment for
And it's only when Americans are affected
That our country even seems to care
While thousands others are STILL dying
Why
Police find "justification" in strangling Eric Garner to death
Why
Yet another young black person gets shot
Oscar Grant
Again
Trayvon Martin

Again
Jordan Davis
Again
Renisha McBride
Again
Michael Brown
WHEN WILL THE VIOLENCE CEASE?!

It's a systematic genocide
And the target is us
No, not just Black people
Not just those in the Middle East
Not even just the minorities or oppressed peoples
It's all of us
Every single last one of us
Tearing each other apart
And we aren't doing anything about it
But locking our doors
And hoping we are not the next criminalized victim
Plastered on the TV screen
And called out of our name

We all live in so much fear...YES FEAR...everyday
That nobody can even enjoy LIFE anymore
What ever happened to walking by faith?
What ever happened to doing unto others
As you would have them do unto you?
Whatever happened to two wrongs don't make a right?
What ever happened to love?

That's our problem
We don't LOVE anymore
Because clearly we don't know what it is anymore
Too many of us are impatient

We don't act kindly
We are jealous of others
So we boast of our accomplishments and in turn are prideful
We are rude and self-centered
And too easily provoked
We keep record of the wrongs of others
Then delight in the evils committed as payback
We don't even know what the truth is
Protection, trust, hope, perseverance
Has all gone away

We're living in a world where
Except for a few of us
We don't love anymore
So maybe for the few of us
I suppose love hasn't failed
(Love never fails, right?)
But the world sure has

For goodness sake
WAKE UP
If three year olds can reconcile differences
Why can't the adults that are supposed to be our leaders
Nobody is "superior" over anybody else
So get over yourselves!
Get rid of all this bitterness and rage and brawling and slander...
Where is our compassion?

#ifidieinpolicecustody

What to Do #ifidieinpolicecustody:

1. When you hear the news
   Be sad
   Be angry
   Be afraid
   It happened to me just like it happened to countless others
   Be ready to take up arms and continue this fight
   For freedom
   For security
   For us
2. When you see my picture
   Make sure it's one of me with my friends
   With my family
   Reading a book
   Graduating
   Smiling
   Doing the things that bright and happy young adults do
   Not the one picture I took
   Where I had a snapback turned to the side
   Throwing a peace sign
   (I'm sorry, a "gang" sign)
   At the camera
3. When they tell you I was in the wrong

Don't believe them
I did not fight them
Except to save my own life
Except to go home safe to my family
Know that I did everything I was supposed to do
I didn't go for their guns or tasers
I didn't talk back
I didn't move my hands off the steering wheel
Unless I warned them first
I pulled over in a well-lit area
I cooperated, I promise
The only crime I committed
Was being a black female
In the wrong place at the wrong time

4. When they try to justify my death based on my previous actions
Don't let them paint me as the bad guy
I am not a thug, a thief, or even a skilled liar
I know that, and you do too
But also do not let them try to say I did not deserve to die
because I'm educated
Or because I grew up in a "good" neighborhood
NO
I did not deserve to die
Because I am a PERSON
And I did nothing wrong

5. When they tell you I did it to myself
Don't believe it
I would never give them the satisfaction of killing myself
I won't bash my own head in
I wouldn't cut myself
I definitely wouldn't shoot myself
And it certainly was no accident
There are no accidents
The official story won't tell you what really happened

Question the circumstances
Until you find some semblance of the truth
6. When they ask you how you know all of this
Tell them that I already had this planned
Just in case the [in]justice system
Tried to take me one day
And turn me into somebody I am not
Know that this is a painful precaution I must take
This hashtag should not exist
It should not have to exist
I should not have to be concerned
Not only with if I was ever murdered
But also what happens to my name after I'm gone
So finally
#IfIDieInPoliceCustody
7.

Speak my name and remember me
Know that I love you all
And that I did everything I could

Invasive

It's back again
Ravaging
Taking over my life
No
Not my life
But his life
But he's part of me
So my life
I'm scared
What will happen
Will it go away
Please say it will
They said they're taking
The least invasive measures
But IT is not
Not to say we have to as well
But why must it be there
Separating perceived
From reality
Why must bad things
Happen to good people
Him
Who makes up half of me
The best friends

The family friends
The people that mean so much
To those that love them
Why must they deal
With the unknown
Disliked
Uncured

Alone

All alone
Even with people who surround me
And bump shoulders with me
Maybe even talk to me
Still alone
Why?
Because you really CAN
Be alone in a crowded room
I have been many times
Too many times

But
I believe there are people
Who are placed in my life
By God
For a reason
People who shared commonalities
In academics or books
Or music styles or personality
Who showed me the meaning
Of being a true friend
Who have been there for me
When nobody else showed up
To the special moments in life

Or who was my hero
When everyone else was
Coming down on me

Being alone happens
Even in the most crowded
Most populated
Of rooms
But I know for a fact that
Thanks to my friends
And the God that gave them to me
I no longer am
Everyone has people
With true purpose
In their lives
To help them through situations
Life may throw at them
The key is to realize
That you don't have to be alone
It's all in the perception

Letting Go

Sometimes the things
That you wanted to be the best
For you
Are only there
For you to give up
In order to see the truly good things
In life

In my life there have been situations
When I was too afraid to let go of
The things I'm comfortable with
The things I like
The things that make me happy

But letting go is all a part of
This life
If it were easy, it wouldn't be
"Letting" go
As in giving yourself permission
To release
If it were easy it would just be taken
Because that requires no decisions
From you

That's hard
It's really tough
To help teenagers with the thing
We struggle with the most
We are much too afraid of change
That we lose sight
Of the ultimate prize
And settle for the mediocre

Even when we know
These things to be true
We still struggle to answer
The biggest question:
Should I stay or let go?

Total Eclipse

This is my first time
Seeing a total eclipse
Smooth black night sky
Deep and rich
Studded with the dazzling stars
Twinkling excitedly
All waiting to see something magnificent

The moon shines
Full, bright, carefree, happy
Such a pristine
And uncontaminated sight
Not a thing
Could extinguish its shine

That is
Until the stars start to disappear
And the sky grows darker
And it's complex dimensionality
Is slammed into 2D
That can only mean one thing
The Fire Nation is attacking

General Zhou and his army

Roll into the sky
And to all but me
Is unbeknownst to the spectators
That still remain
They have no idea
Just how dangerous this guy is

In one fell swoop he steals the moon spirit
And crushes it with his bare hands
The yin and yang
Can no longer swim in harmony
Yin is gone
Yang swims in chaotic circles
And the moon grows angry
And removes its pristine mask
And exposes the inner fire
It already had burning inside

Angry red envelopes the moon
My moon
Exposing its deep inner pain
Its secrets it has held in for so long
I look around to see who else
Is seeing this
But the other spectators
Have come to believe
That the moon has just been
Covered up for a while
That bright orb is it's true form
The red is only a cool mask

They're wrong
When I look I see the moon's sadness
As it mourns over its crushed spirit

It's desperation
As it seeks Katara
For her healing hands
Or Yue
To restore his spirit back
Or maybe even the Avatar
So he can kick General Zhou's butt

But nobody appears
Nobody can save the moon
From the Fire Nation burns
It has endured
The moon's searching eyes find me
And see that I can see it's pain
And it's scarred red body
But doesn't allow himself to cry
In front of me

He slowly replaces his shining
Bright white happy mask
And the stars come back into view
And see that he has been
"Uncovered"
That nothing blocks his way anymore
That the red was a spectacular
Trick of the light

As the others leave
I remain behind
And watch the moon as it
Returns to its usual fullness
Til it's smiling such a flashy smile
That nobody could even imagine
That he was attacked by the Fire Nation

And that he's hurting
And hiding behind that mask

To most
The moon is two-dimensional orb
Happy bright shining all the time
But I know what resides in its depth
Because for a moment
I caught a glimpse of the complexity
That lies inside
I have seen the blood of the moon

Sitting in the Dark

He opens the door for me finally
And lets me in
He turns the music back up
And sits at his desk
And doesn't say a word
His shirt is off
And a permanent scowl etched on his face
And it is dark

The only light comes from the computer screen
That illuminates the anger
And the hurt
On his face

I too take out my laptop
Attempting to appear as if
I am not watching his every move
But I am

The music fills the darkness
With the sounds of pain
And anger
Of wishing for a new life
Of wishing for a quick end

Of drinking away your troubles
Of never wanting to say goodbye

His screen goes dark
And the songs of his current life cease
And he lays his head on the bed
And nothing can be heard from him
But his breathing coming slow and hard

I close my laptop
And I melt into the darkness
And watch him wrestle with his emotions
Careful to only move when necessary
To breathe as softly as I can
As if I am not even there

But internally I know I want to do something
Other than just watch him
I want to jump off the bed
And hug him
And not let him go
Until his hurt disappears for the time
I want to hold his hand
And let him know that
I am here
I see you
I love you
I want to help you

But I am frozen
Frozen in my assumptions
That he will be okay
He needs to let it out for himself
Knowing that not doing something

Will only bring regrets
Yet still I sit
Watching
As his pain shows itself
Sitting in the dark

Am I Stupid?

He called me stupid
He said that I was a blabbermouth
And I didn't know what I was doing
And I was an idiot
And I was nosy
And he never wanted to see me again
He said if something happened to him it would be my fault
And I believed every word
Even after he apologized
And got a chance to calm down
And told me didn't really mean it
He did at some point.
He did too mean it
If only for a time
The thoughts had to come from somewhere
He doesn't trust me anymore
He never really trusted me
He doesn't trust anyone
He didn't really hit me
But his words were a slap to the face

I'm to blame
I did it
I'm in the wrong

It's all my fault

He wouldn't do that

He loves me

He wants me

He only wants me

Right?

RIGHT?

It's not fair

I'm supposed to be your one and only

And instead of it being my fault

It's YOURS

YOU did this

You did this to me and to us

It hurts

It hurts

I can never look at another text or random phone call the same

anymore

I will forever be paranoid that you are talking to whoever it was

I'm always concerned with what you're doing

Sad when you don't acknowledge me or when I think I make you

mad

You think you have trust issues

I hate to say that now I do too

I'm so pitiful

I just wanna cry

And scream

And run away

Run fast and hard and get away from all the pain of

Feeling yet again

Like I am not good enough

I'm new at this

I'm naïve

So

Stupid
I don't wanna feel like this anymore
I want to be secure in my own relationship
I want to know he's really here for me
I want to know he's faithful to me and only me
I gotta stay true to myself
But I'm not even sure who I am anymore
I'm just really lost

"What's Up With You?"

I walked back to my room while holding it in with every step

And doing my best not to break into a run.

I held it together until I got into my room

And slammed the door shut.

That slam was my starter signal

For all the tears

I had held in for so long.

Broken

Your first love
The world is shining and is sparkling
Prisms rainbow splitting
Soft lap of gentle waves
Sun-kissed breeze, tender touch
You laugh together and complete each other
That piece of you that will never be replaced
You were a pair that was really just one that couldn't be separated
You got lost in each other's eyes and smiles
You hold hands and sing along to songs on the radio
You make each other laugh
You kiss and hold each other tightly
And you never think of having to let them go
But you weren't ready to take them on
And they weren't ready for you either
You both were so innocent and new
To this particular union of hearts
You both had your own struggles
That didn't come to light
Until much after you said those three words
That even still mean all the world to you

First emergence of trouble
Not because you are bad people

You are people who have held in their emotions
And have bottled up their fears
And have taken on a lot in this world
And are just now realizing
That they should've fixed this before
They realized that they have problems
And they see the other's problems
And they want to go help the other person patch up their holes
Neglecting their own
Not realizing they are the only ones
That can patch up their own holes for good
Not seeing the troubles
Splashing over their feet and rising to their ankles and calves
Swaying them to and fro
Covering the sun and the light
Whipping the winds around to lash at their faces
They cling desperately to each other
Not wanting to be lost in this now raging sea of troubles and hurt
That is reaching is boiling point
Their holes are gushing
Irreparable
Uncontainable
Love and hurt are all intertwining

Breaking point
Eruption of waves crashing
Hot gushing wet slap across the face
Stinging bitter salty in your eyes
Hurt crashing waves down over you
Troubles explode with a furious heat
Agony and pain ripping
Through the very fabric that has stitched you together
Until all you have are threads
And you try to hold on

Desperately
Because the world is ending

But you can't

You break
And you scream as you are carried away from each other
The realization that your heart cannot take it
Hits you in the chest
The million pieces of your shattered heart
Firing like shrapnel lodging into your lungs
And you gasp for air
Even long after the waves have subsided
And the winds are gone
And an eerie calm has settled
Gasping you struggle to your feet
Confused
Questioning
Broken
Still barely breathing
Wondering what just happened
And knowing that he is too

Lonely
Nothing in the world makes sense anymore
Walk around confused
But don't show it
Seeing him, but not recognizing him anymore
You slowly start to mend your hearts
Mend your holes
Move forward
Wondering if you're ever going to be whole again
Knowing that you won't really be

You remember
You remember the gentle kiss
You remember the whispered secrets
That only the two of you could tell
Because they're the missing piece
And you both know it
But are you ready to put them back there?
Will you ever be?
Or will your love remain forever separated
And though it is there
You still have it for each other
Will it forever stay broken?

Again

There it is again
That notion
That idea
That hurtful accusation
You say you have trust issues
You don't care that I'm trying
You don't care what I say
No matter what I do you're
Angry
Jealous
Hurt
Mistrusting
You don't trust me but you say you love me
And I don't understand that at all
How can you ask me if I'll protect your heart
But all you do is bash down mine
How is it that you can express your anger
When you shut me down when I express mine
I'm not even angry often
Heck for you I try not to be angry at all
But I am
You say there is a rage building up inside of you?
I'm scared
I don't want to go back to that place

Where we argue all the time
And I can't seem to think for myself
Or reason for myself
Where all I care about is you

Broken Too

The aftermath of being broken
Is by far worse than the break itself
So much confusion in between
Not knowing what is okay anymore
Not knowing anything anymore

My heart is so fragile
Like a recovering patient
Susceptible to complications
Like a recovering addict
Going through withdrawals
My heart is still missing that piece
That I will never get back

Sometimes it's still hard to breathe
Because those puncture wounds are still in my lungs
When I see him my heart flutters
But I no longer know
If I am happy to see him
Or if my fight or flight defenses are kicking in

Every time I want to cry again when I think about
What COULD HAVE been
But I know that it wasn't meant to be

Not right now
Not for me
It hurts so bad
My heart twisting my soul into
Complicated knots
Tangling up my mind
Until doing anything at all becomes
Darn near impossible
My life has fallen into disarray
I tried so hard to be my best
But my best also means
That it hurts the most
To be so distant and separated from you
When I want to be so close again

I know that I need to be away to allow my heart to heal
But it makes it all the harder to know
That we will never be the same again
There's a hole that will never be mended

I don't want to feel like this again
But who's to say this isn't like a vaccination
Inoculation against another heartbreak
So maybe if it ever happens again
I can withstand it more
I never knew they were so right
When they said that the first breakup
Is always the hardest

Love is so wonderful
But when you lose it
And you can't get it back the same way
It does something to you
Life doesn't feel the same anymore

Melodramatic? Maybe a little
But it's true
Or maybe it's the longing for everything to be okay again
That's changing my outlook
Either way
I so badly want this mending
This healing
I miss being whole

What happens when you get over them anyways
DO you mend that hole?
That will be the day
Yet I still get the suspicious feeling
That even when your heart moves on
Even when you can breathe again
There is a scar left
That will never be like it used to be
And at the center of that scar
Is that piece he still holds
That I will never get back

Not Again

That look
Shit
I did it again
Said something I KNOW I shouldn't have even mentioned
And in front of our friends too
Shit
Now he's angry, and I deserve every bit of wrath
Why can't I keep my mouth shut
Why do I have to bring up those things
Why do I have to be such an idiot
Why can't I be the good
Trustworthy
Loyal
And loving woman I was supposed to be
Instead I keep hurting him
And reminding him of things
That happened in the past
And that he couldn't control
It's so out of my place to say those things
I feel horrible
I didn't mean to strike that nerve
Every time something is going well
We reach some sort of understanding
And then suddenly I say something horrible

And hurt him

And cut deep

And now I'm afraid

He hasn't spoken to me yet

He told me that hurt and then stopped talking to me

He's being friendly with everyone else in the room

But he doesn't even look up

I know I screwed up again

I didn't mean it!!!

I don't even know why I was compelled to say that!

It just came out

That's no excuse though

I screwed up and betrayed his trust AGAIN

When will I learn

When will I be better

When will I stop getting myself into these situations

Now I'm stuck

And he's upset

And I still don't even know why I said it

That isn't even something you joke about

Why would I say that in front of everyone

That was between us

I shouldn't even want other people to know that

Because while the thing itself made me sad

I do understand why it happened

And I just acted like I didn't care about his feelings at all

Now he's probably going to vent to his bros

And it's another strike against me

I feel sick to my stomach

And dizzy

And not well overall

I'm sorry

He doesn't even want to hear that

I really am sorry though

I feel like crap
I should know him better than most everyone else
On this campus
But I treat him horribly when it comes to telling his business
I don't have any special privileges for being his girl
Am I even still?
I haven't smiled since I said it either
I'm sorry
I'm sorry
I'm sorry
Please please please I didn't mean to say that
I can't live with this
I hate to upset him like this
I know there are times when he gets upset over
Something that I can't fix
But I can fix me
I really can
I can

Is This How She Felt?

Is this how she felt
Always seeing and hearing
About another
Who seemed to come from nowhere
And take his time
And his attention
And eventually his heart
Did he tell her
That he loved her
But then praise the other
Did she get jealous
Did she think he was slipping away
Through her fingers
And nothing she could do
The other was just so great
And wonderful
That he wanted the other instead
Did she feel afraid
And insecure
Did she do desperate things
And try to hold onto him
Because she wanted his love
And attention back
When he disappeared with her

And never really even
Introduced them?
Cuz if this is how she felt
Then I'm in big trouble

Can You See?

Do you know what it feels like
To be selectively invisible
And I don't mean I decided one day that
I was going to choose when the world saw me
I mean it was something forced upon me
Someone else decided that's what I was

Can you see her
The girl hidden away in the corner
Shrinking into herself every time she
Is touched
Shiver running down her spine
A familiar anxiety creeping into her bones
Jumping every time someone speaks to her
Rush of adrenaline making her wish she could move
Get away
She is frightened

I was already a wallflower
Growing up on the periphery
I didn't like attention drawn to myself
Nobody really paid much attention
Past my initial transplantation
I was pushed aside

Left to my own devices
Not too many people care about a wallflower

Can you see the prints left around her neck
Of someone's hands who never touched her
Who never had to touch her
But whose words are etched into her soul
Reminding her at even the slightest movement
That she is marked
She is not her own

Can you see the trails of tears she never let fall
For fear of bringing the weight of the world
Crashing down onto her
None of this is her fault and yet

I wish someone would have seen me
I wish someone would have believed me
Seeing is believing

Invisible Bruises

I know you can't see
The angry red handprints
Around my neck
He put them there
When he told me he loved me
And would kill himself if I left
He cracked my ribcage open
And left my heart exposed
For him to stick pins into
Like his personal pincushion
When he said that he cheated on me
Because I wasn't doing enough
To please him
He slapped my face
Repeatedly
Everytime he told me
That all of our problems
Were my fault

It's hard not to see it as my fault
When that is what gets beaten into me
With every glance
Every frown that stays only between us
Every sigh that tells me

He is angry
I shouldn't have said that
The mask of smiles that he put up for our friends
While he is making fun of me
So innocent to them
But so dangerous for me
I dare not show him my discontent
I cannot embarrass him in public

He steps on my fingers
And grinds my joints into dust
When he tells me not to tell anyone
About what happens in our relationship
Breaking me down
Into a small
Worthless
Silent
Heap

He socked me in the stomach until I was gasping
And begging him to stop
As he threatened to end our relationship
If I didn't cut the ties
To my only support systems
He wanted me all to himself
He said he loved me

My black eye is from the gaslighting
The split lip is from the name-calling
My broken femur is from the weight
Of all his constant lies
My dislocated elbow is from being used
As his emotional punching bag
The scarred and scraped and tender knees

Came from the belittling that always yanked me
To the ground beneath him
The gash across my neck from his coercion to perform acts
That I did not consent to
And the bullet through my face
Is from the damage and the harm caused
By his cruel laugh and crooked smile
That nobody but I could see

His words always cutting deep
His looks gutting me down to the bone
But although blood is pooling in my chest
And spilling out of my eyes
And tracking down my cheeks
And I am sobbing
And I can't breathe
Still nobody can see anything wrong with me

A Way Out

It was April 20th, 2015. I stood rocking on the balls of my feet on the sidewalk, the breeze from the passing cars whipping around my face as I stared into the oncoming traffic. The headlights only somewhat registered as I hesitantly lifted my foot to take another step towards the asphalt. For the first time in a long time, I was perfectly calm. My heart was beating normally and my hands weren't shaking and I didn't have the sudden urge to cry or run away. My mind was fairly blank, so I just stared into the shadows and patterns of light made by the passing cars. I shuffled another pace further. I was completely lost.

Someone who I thought was a friend had come up to me outside of my dorm and told me a bunch of rumors he'd heard about me, and that he believed every one of them. Even worse, he told me that several of my other friends believed them as well. I attempted to tell him that the rumors weren't true, and to open up about what was really going on, but he dismissed me and left me standing alone on the sidewalk in the dark. Something in me broke entirely. *Nobody believes me...*I felt the tightness in my chest rising up. *Nobody believes me...*fear was gripping my mind. *Nobody believes me...*I wanted a way out. I was still standing outside of my building when I looked over at the busy street and suddenly my mind came up with a way out. I became eerily calm, but I didn't feel in control; I barely felt like myself at all. I had lost the sense of being Destinee. After my mind had endured that dissonance for a whole year, I simply couldn't do it anymore.

Things Never Said Beyond the Lights

When I was standing on the balcony
Eyes wide
Chest heavy
Fragile fragments of my soul
Floating in pieces outside of myself
Strained and stabbed and jagged
Cutting into my heart
Pooling blood carrying me downward
Like a relentless gravity
And you watched me try to jump
Fly, soar *free* and find my *way*
Because I didn't realize
That was not the *way*
To *free* myself
And you.......
You caught me
And held me
And told me
"I see you"
And I looked into your eyes and I saw that hope
That you say you never speak of
But you let seep out from the cracks in your exterior *anyway*

And some of it splashed onto me
And you pulled me to safety
I never said how much
Your presence that day
Was like the happy ever after
I didn't think I would get

But now
In your distance and your silence
I want to ask you
No now I need to know
If you really saw me

See because when you are afraid of what you are seeing before you
You heart and your mind start to
Race and
You're thinking quickly on your toes
Not wanting to be the cause of a tragedy
And when you tell me that you see me
Do you see the hurt or do you see me
Because in that moment I just needed
Some affirmation of my existence at all
But now I have come to depend on you
And I thought you would always be there for me
And I thought that whenever I needed you
I could reach out
And grab a hold of you
Your strength would reaffirm my own
Wrapping me in a security blanket

And I wanted you to see my tears
Because the darkness that lies beyond the lights
Is what frightens me most
And I thought you were my light

To shine on in the scariness
But the thing is you never said
That this frightened you too

But I question if you ever saw that darkness
Or if you only wanted to be the light
Meaning you only wanted to be the hero
Meaning that you get to live out your fantasy stories
Meaning that you are always the person that people depend on
To save them from themselves
And you have no investment in me
Me

Can't you see who the fuck I am
I am me and I don't know if you know who that is
Because if you did ....
You would actually try
You would try to see me
Because right **now** I don't know if you are trying
Because maybe you would've answered my call

So I'm leaving you this message
To say that I didn't jump
I found my own light
I left the balcony
And I don't need you to save me
I just wanted you to want me forreal

3

Rising

The Beauty in Self Discovery

I love to see the wonder
Of a phoenix being born out of the ashes
Or a lotus rising from the mud

Here was the magic of creation
Born out of a second chance
At finding my own
Destinee

My Deepest Fear

Our deepest fear is not that we are inadequate
Our deepest fear is that we are powerful beyond measure
Powerful words from a powerful poem
That talks about the power in us
And inspires us not to be afraid of us
Except
My deepest fear is that I am nothing of that sort
My deepest fear is that I am inadequate
My deepest fear is that I am weak beyond repair
My darkness is what frightens me
Because my light has gotten so dim
I can't see much beyond my own face
Who AM I to be brilliant gorgeous talented and fabulous?
I don't seem to have a right to be
Yes, I am a child of God
But sometimes I feel so alone
And helpless and hurt and I wonder
What sort of plan He actually has for me
When I get out of this mess?
My playing small doesn't serve the world
But it serves me
Nobody feels insecure around me
So it should be okay if I shrink
Maybe if I make myself small enough

The world won't hurt me so bad
I want to shine as children do
But where's my light
Everyone expecting me to act like an adult
Be less optimistic and more realistic
Think for myself but don't be selfish
Handle myself, fix it myself
Have taken my childlike light away
I can only hope there is still the glory of God in me
It is supposed to be in everyone
I can only hope and pray that one day
My light will shine again
And I can show others that you can pick yourself up
And stand on your own two feet
You can rebuild your life
You can overcome the darkness
You can shine on your own
And you can say that your deepest fear
Is
That you are powerful beyond measure
Or better yet
That you aren't afraid of yourself at all
Because you are powerful beyond measure
And there's nothing anyone can do
To take that away from you again
Cause can't nobody
Take your joy
Can't nobody steal your love
And nobody
NOBODY
Should ever make you feel afraid
Or like you are too powerful
Cause chances are, you're holding back
Of course saying is easier than doing

One day my actions
Will actually line up with my words
But until then
I haven't yet been liberated from my own fear

Not Black Enough

A Letter from the Black Girl to the World
It's amazing how the superficial
Skin-deep things are all that matter to you
You say I'm half there, an almost Black
Well I've got news for you
I'm Black enough to feel threatened too
When my brothers and sisters go through some BS
That threatens them
Because I'm Black enough to know what it means
To be so intricately complicatedly connected
To everyone in my community
One neuron being cut in this network
Makes the others seize and quake
Firing haywire in order to compensate for the loss
Regardless of what part of the brain they all come from
I'm Black enough to know
How messed up it is to try to act "not suspicious"
(Which also suggests that I have something to constantly
Be suspicious about)
My stomach doing flips when I walk into a store
Or down the street
Or in the dark
But flashing that smile and radiating pleasantness *anyway*
Because I don't have time or energy to get stopped today

I'm Black enough for my amygdala to be constantly activated
Adrenaline always poised ready to move in
Regardless of where I stand
KKK sounding like three gunshots vibrating my ear drum
Until I am sure it will rupture
Fear is real, it always has been it always will be
And you have never known a fear like this
Until you step into your own skin
And realize that nothing you ever do is enough
To be of value to everyone else
You don't care that I'm a college student
You don't care that can speak or write well
You don't care that I consider myself to be successful
Or that I have goals and dreams
You mistake my intelligence for a crutch that somehow
Holds me above my race
But it doesn't matter that I'm smart if you can't see my brilliance
In my darkness
Not your "milk's favorite cookie" type of darkness
Where all you want is to strip me of my outsides
Clean away all the dirt
And expose your sweet white filling inside
I mean all of my darkness
Why can't you see that this is such an integral part of me
Like the stars studded in the sky
My radiance accentuates the night, it's there
And I can't escape it

I'm Black enough to have my heart broken over and over
And over again
Spilling blood into my insides and flooding my being with despair
Every time I see the way you treat other people who look
Just like me

Like the high school girls
Who were thrown around by cops this year
Like the little kids who were shot and killed this year
Like the countless students that were threatened
Just for being Black this year
Like my little brother, who is a young Black man
Who's my right hand
Who's still coming into his own this year
Don't you tell me I'm not Black enough!
I've got the heartbreak and the tearstains
And the fear and the anger
The apparent invisibility that comes with inhabiting this body
I AM BLACK I won't change that no matter what
The least you can do is acknowledge that I am
Enough

Another Race Poem

This summer I was yet again disappointed in
Our injustice system
Shots fired
Shots fired
No policemen fired
Who knew Black and blue were such *incompatible* colors?

This is not a race poem
Because in a race poem
I talk about what it's like to be Black in America
But with the way our existence is being threatened
I feel like fewer and fewer people
Can actually say
What it's like to be Black in America
In a race poem
I point out the differences in Black and Not
But clearly everyone already knows the difference
Because Black is leaving their bodies on the pavement
And Not is paid leave
Black is still asking for freedom
And Not is notably free

I'm supposed to talk about how I feel
But I can't

Not that I can't talk about it
But there is nothing there in my heart to talk about
My mind tells me I should mourn
So I *try* to mourn
I *try* to write
I *try* to sing
But everything is numb
I whisper to my body where does it hurt
And it says nowhere
Nowhere

Now here is the predicament I face
When I get back to campus
And I want my peers to understand
This numb
This pain
And I march and I yell
And cry from the depths of my soul
But when you look into my face
The only question that forms on your lips
Seeks *my* validation of *your* privileged existence
I am angry, sad, hurt, confused
Numb
Numb
Numb
How can a group of hurting people
Lay their souls bare in front of everyone
During the most tumultuous time on our campus
And you trample over our souls
As easily as you walk up onto the campus circulator
And let that White vesicle take you everywhere you need to go

I can't write another race poem
I've tried to say what I needed to say

When I screamed that I am enough
When I laid out a plan for what to do if I died in police custody
When I questioned where the love has gone
I can't write another race poem
Not because it hurts so bad
But because I don't know how to say

That

This is not a race poem
This is the poem of a young Black woman with **insomnia**

What It's Like to Be an Over-Analyzer

What it's like to be an over-analyzer
(for those of you who aren't)
It's tossing and turning in the middle of the night
Completely incapable of sleeping because
There's so much weighing on your mind
And finally when you've had enough
Getting up out of bed
And calling your friends at 2 in the morning to ask
If they were mad at you two weeks ago
And hearing the silence
And for a moment being terrified
That they're going to say that YES
That look they gave you as they passed you on campus
Two weeks ago
When you thought maybe they didn't see you
Was because they were mad at you and they question
How you could even be so stupid
As to calling them your friend now
But then
Feeling extra bad when they say no
Of course not
And they hang up

And you start to wonder
...Are they mad at you now?

It's that over-cautious feeling
Like walking through a glass shop
Its pristine smoothness pressing upon you
Hiding its shards within the bounds of its shine
And being afraid to breathe
Because you're convinced that taking one breath
Will completely disrupt the equilibrium of the air in the room
All the molecules rapidly descending into complete chaos
Running into the glass and loosening its shards
The vibrations of my fearful shivering
Stemming from the knowledge that
I've caused a catastrophe
By simply living and breathing and taking up space
Causing cataclysmic side-effects, which would be, of course
That the glass would just explode and shatter into a million
Tiny irreparable pieces

It's when you make a bad decision
Like when you decide to stay with a guy
That you say you love
Even though he manipulates your emotions
And makes everything already working overtime in your head
Work harder
And you know that all of this is wrong because you see
That look in your eyes every time you look in the mirror
And you just know that you should leave...
And then you stay because
You thought that things were going to get better somehow
But he just continued to hurt you over and over again
And your heart drops into your toes
Because you feel like you should've seen that coming

Because you *are* the most analytical person you know

It's having your best friend tell you
That it's okay to take a leap of faith
And there's nothing to worry about
And not really believing him but agreeing anyways
Because for the most part your friends don't understand
The hazard that is your head and heart
Making an attempt to work together
They don't see how much of a struggle it is
To take a leap of faith when you can't clearly see the outcome
When your head keeps coming up with the worst
Yet possible scenarios for everything
And your heart wants you to try anyways
And you know you seem indecisive
When really

It's knowing deep down in your heart
That you are the best person in the world
To make decisions about you
For you
But you still aren't quite sure
And you're never quite sure

It's being confident
And having no way to prove it

Release

I never really understood
The saying
To wear my heart on my sleeve
My heart is not on my sleeve
My heart usually stays in my chest
Thudding out the rhythm of my life
Keeping in time
With the band of situations
That have shaped me
Into the composition before you

But sometimes
Parts of my heart do leak out a little
Not to my sleeve
No there isn't enough space there
My heart shows on my face
The very pages of my existence
Racing down
Sharp defined streaks
Matching the sharp turn
Sharp key of the notes of my life
Low rumbling up from the very pit
Of my soul
Spilling over the edge

Vibrato
Until I am unable to contain
The tears in my sheet music
The tears
The *tears*

Sweet riffs turned salty
At the icy cold timbre
That had become my life
Frozen
Unable to play another note
For fear of playing it wrong
I stood
Looking up at the rips and shreds
Of my music
My life
Coming down all around me

C'mon Destinee
Just try again
You'll get it this time
No you don't understand
My band director is so
Metronomically meticulous
Of how I play my music
He'll be angry if I don't play it how he wants
I know I should just play
My own song
But there is so much pressure
To constantly be performance ready, I
Fall flat
On my face
And he beat—beat—beats me down
Throws my insecurities around

Like a baton conducting which way I should go
Even when I don't want to go there

I can't handle this stage
Of my life
So many unknowns
I'm sight-reading in the dark
I can't get enough air
To play the notes
I'm gasping
I'm lost
I'm the little girl
Who forgot how to play
Her own song

One wrong note turns into two
Three four
Or is it six eight?
Whole notes
Being cut time
And time again
Spiraling down into this dark hole
Cacophony
The pitch overwhelms me
I can't take it anymore

So I play the only song I still know

The song that comes from
The bass of my hurts
Treble trills my loves
And passions
From everything that makes me
Sweet sassy saxophone Destinee

The cover to *my* heart
Roll, ebb, flow
I let the waves of harmony glisten on my cheeks
Until I've been scaled back to a more natural tempo

When most people hear the harmony
And they don't know my melody
It's almost like they're offended I'm there
Playing anything at all
I can't always play the melody
I'm not always first chair
My fingers get all twisted up and
My inability to play is alarming
Sometimes I have to run away
Run, go play my harmony to myself

And
That's okay
Because without the moments where the harmony comes in
The melody is nothing
Some of the most important measures of life
Are also the moments of the greatest
Release

Worldview

Change
My whole existence is encapsulated by change
I pack the pieces of my life up
And they never quite fit the same
When I get to my destination
Cognitive dissonance making me
Cognitively diss my stance
On the world I have experienced for so long

Crying, for instance, used to be for babies
Or whiners
Or I guess the people who were too weak
To handle their position in this world
Something to look down upon
Activism was yelling and screaming and frightening
And angry...always angry
When people forced their views on others
And were not fair to those around them
Holding hands was a sign that you were immature
Too little to make it on your own
Having to rely on someone bigger, stronger
Separation—that's how you counteracted that one
Striking it off on your own
Proving yourself

Love?
Only reserved for significant others
And moms and dads
And favorite books and TV shows and chocolate
And maybe siblings
And you know, siblings are under the constraints of
Sharing your flesh and blood
Who grew up in your house and shared your stuff
Until they didn't
And then that love comes into question

I didn't know of any experiences
That could possibly change how I thought
Thinking is eternal and everlasting
And you always are however you came
And I just didn't realize
How misconstrued my vision of the world was

That is until I experienced my first real heartbreak
And every subsequent heartbreak after that
And the times where my heart felt so full I thought it would burst
All the love I've experienced by the people that I love
And who love me
But I didn't know that love could exist in all the ways that it does
Support, care, a hand to hold, a shoulder to cry on
Something real and tangible to fight for
Suddenly nothing was as it seemed
My life was much more complicated
Than some jaded definitions of what it means to be
A person

How could I be so ignorant to think
That only roses are red and only violets are blue
My view is not stationary

Heck, neither is the world
Constantly turning, circling
Finding new angles
And never quite being the same
Each time it makes its way around the sun

I am this world
Constantly spinning and shifting
And becoming a new version of myself
Never flat
Dynamic

Nostalgia

Nostalgia
When you recognize that you are metamorphasizing
And transforming into the person you always were inside
And you think about who you were when you first got to college
High school
Middle school
And you smile
Because you remember your awkward phases and phrases
And the people you were with and the things that you did
And you are different now
You are adult

But it's that hunch in your shoulders when you pause on the word
Adult
Are you adult?
Does your concept of an adult even have the same meaning
As it did before you realized that you were one?

This transformation is uncomfortable

Putting your feet in mommas heels
And realizing that they actually fit you now
This isn't dress up anymore, this is real life
Doing taxes is hard

Paying bills is hard
Adulting is really hard
And yet
When you are finally sitting at the grown up table
When your opinion matters
Loving the feeling of being an adult
But even so wishing times were simpler again
When the hardest decision you had to make
Was what color you chose out of the crayon box next

Maybe that's why college students revert back
To our childlike ways
Watching marathon after marathon of Aang and Goku
And Virgil Ovid Hawkins
What's the sitch, gotta catch 'em all, and TRUUDDYYYY
Repopulating our lexicon
Fantasies of getting slimed
Or riding on the Magic School Bus returning
Every theme song we thought long forgotten
Popping right back into our heads
As soon as we hear even a hint of the first notes

Going hard in games of capture the flag
Trying (and sometimes failing) at bike and skateboard tricks
Having snowball fights and building snowmen
Seeing if you can still double dutch
Like Keke Palmer and Corbin Bleu
Sitting out on grassy hills or climbing trees
Or playing frisbee
(though now it's called ultimate, that makes it cooler)
Making chalk drawings on the sidewalk
And going to the Residential College Olympics
So we have an excuse to play
Releasing the anxiety that came

With our greater sense of self-awareness
That we'd acquired in the past decade

And we smile

We all remember the days of wanting to be an adult
But we're starting to reach that point
Where we want to be like children
Again
Back when we really believed that we could fly
If we tried hard enough
And there are times it twists your stomach into knots
Because who likes letting go?
But I'd say that's all part of the metamorphosis
We are still becoming who we are, and sometimes who we are
Involves who we were
Growth is not a rejection of the things in the past
Growth is figuring out where to place them in our present
And never forgetting

One More Chapter

They tell you to never judge a book
By its cover
Instead to pick it up and see
If the content of its pages can compensate
For any lack of exterior qualities

But most of the time
If the book has a cover that is plain
Or the title isn't immediately eye catching
We toss it to the side without so much as a second glance
Destined to be a book that never gets out of the
"Might read" pile

But why not read *that* book
That absorbs you into its pages
Where the rest of the world disappears
If only for a moment
These treasure troves seem only to be found
In the stories that you never imagined reading

They don't seem like much externally
But the inside is a world of wonder
This is the one that keeps you company in the glow of a flashlight
Under the covers

This is the one that comes before anything else
This is the one you know will always be by your side
Because you can never escape the beauty it holds within
Even when you tell yourself you'll be done with this chapter
You always convince yourself to read
Just one more

And you fall
You fall for the way the words tumble across the page
Like they have no cares for where they go next
As long as you're there together
The spine holding together the masterpiece
The cover a locked door and you have the key
To unlock the hidden gems
That make it all worthwhile
Every turn of the page is a risk
A blind leap into the unknown
Where the possibilities are endless
And you've decided that now
You are invested
And being invested is having faith
That the author knew what she was doing

And then one day you're there
When everything is looking up
Like happily ever after is approaching
And you turn the page
And the next chapter is non-existent
Only an epilogue and a few choice words about the author
Maybe some questions to ponder for your book club

This is where falling in love stops being like reading a novel
Novels have a beginning a middle and an end
On a loop contained within the boundaries

Of its pre-determined page limits
I don't want love to have a page limit
I want to take a pen
And write out the remainder to my own story
Where the book is only part one of an endless series
I want to fill a library

So that one day
I am sitting down in a big comfy love seat
An open book on my lap
Reading the tales of
How the love story of a lifetime can transcend
The simple paper thin boundaries meant to contain us

He sees the empty pages towards the end
And he takes out his favorite pen with a knowing smile
And asks me

One more chapter?

Rebirth of a Phoenix

I am living this life
Knowing I will eventually crumble to ashes
My body will fall apart
Piece by piece
Catastrophic and devastating
Bursting into flames
The fire of life consuming me
Until I am nothing left

I know this
Because I have lived it
And as in many great cycles in life
I know that I am destined to live it
Again

I have experienced the crumbling
My first time in the ashes
Where it's dark and its cold
And my heart has turned to stone
Nobody recognizes me
I am hidden away
In the recesses
Of my own sorrows
Ash and smoke filling my lungs

Breathing hurts
My sight is diminished
And my own blindness is painful

I loved my former form
Beautifully innocent sweet flame
Enveloping my every movement
Never burning anyone else
Lavender fire in my eyes
Gentleness and caring
Dominant within me
Lovely young phoenix
Never knowing her own gentle fire
Could get her burned

Such is life
That we go through changes
It conflicts and makes
Your own head and heart
Rebel

It is this rebellion
That sent me spiraling down into
My dark oblivion
My feathers falling away
Plummeting out of the sky
Til I am only a heap
Of an essence
Of myself
My essence wanted so much more
From the circumstances
I was dealt
I couldn't be ashes forever

From that essence
Began a new fire
Bold and striking
Deep reds and golds and orange
Erupting out of the ash
Drawing together every ounce
Of my being
Into a fiery and gorgeous
And confident me
Where my fire is a powerful coat
Protecting and keeping me
Those negative experiences retreating to a safe distance
For fear of being burned

My eyes a deep royal purple
Sure and strong
Still gentle and caring
But I have grown to love
My new fire and
My new colors and
My life
And
Me

I am not afraid anymore
To stumble upon ashes
Because I know that no matter the
Darkness
Pain
I will emerge stronger
Even more beautiful
And with the knowledge of how to cope with my own
Insecurities and fears
And nothing will be able to convince me

That my own power will not be enough
Because I am more than enough
And growing every day

The rebirth of a phoenix
Is a journey into my own liberation

Acknowledgements

My first and biggest thank you goes to God, my Creator and the reason for the life I am living. Without Him, I truly do not believe I would be here and able to write the pieces of this story to share it with all of you.

Thank you to my parents and my brother who helped me to see this vision through in whatever ways they could. You are always my biggest cheerleaders (and proofreaders)—I couldn't have done this without you.

Thank you to my INCREDIBLE graphic designer who allowed my phoenix to literally take flight. This cover is my new favorite work of art and I will cherish the time, effort, and care you put into it.

Thank you to my friends who challenged me to write poetry in the first place, who supported me in my poetry slams and open mic nights, who made sure my mental health was okay, who kept me fed when I ran out of meal points on campus, who let me sleep on their couches when I was too anxious to go back to my dorm at night, who believed me when I said I'd been hurt before I could articulate that I'd been abused, who encouraged me to go to therapy and applauded me when I finally did, who nudged me to write and release this story in this format, who showed me *how* to release this in this format, who head my fan club, and finally who accepted me as I am and continue to love on me. You all have helped make this journey worthwhile and I am forever grateful to all of you.

Thank you to all of the readers who have stories similar to mine and have never told anyone. You aren't alone.

Thank you to all of the readers who have ever been on a journey of self-discovery. I wrote this for you as much as I wrote this for me.

Destinee has written poetry since late in high school when one of her friends challenged her to write free verse poetry that didn't rhyme, thus breaking her ideas of what poetry could be. She realized that she loved how through poetry she could be her fullest self and finally express the thoughts swirling in her head. That love came in handy during college when she faced many struggles including self-doubt and mental illness, and was entangled in an abusive relationship. Writing gave her stability while her world was in chaos, and upon reflection, showed her just how chaotic her world had become. Poetry was also her way out of that darkness and back into the light of her self-discovery and self-love.

Destinee lives in Atlanta, GA and is a medical student at Morehouse School of Medicine. Her dream is to help people to reach their fullest potentials so that they can be the best version of themselves. In sharing her story and her experience, she hopes that she has been able to fulfill some of that dream.

Also by Destinee Shipley

Destinee is one of many featured BIPOC poets in an anthology by the collective, Protest Through Poetry.

Protest Through Poetry Anthology

 Protest Through Poetry is an international collective of BIPOC activist poets. The anthology materialized after PTP's digital seminar on the intersection of poetry and activism. In solidarity, we read, wrote, and shared poetry, being present with one another as an act of political resistance. This anthology is a physical manifestation of our collective protest against injustice. May these words disrupt, empower, heal, and make our stories visible.